How To Win Friends And Influence Google

Marketing For Small Business In The Age Of Search Engines

Get Your Local Business
Ranked at the Top of Google

Mike Griffin
http://www.LouisvilleMarketingLabs.com

Contents

Introduction

A few years ago, at the 2007 Strategic Advertising Summit, Microsoft mogul, Bill Gates, predicted yellow pages usage would drop to near zero by the year 2012 for people under the age of 50. Gates' prediction seems to be coming true as the yellow pages are beginning to see double digit declines in advertising sales, as their former users are now turning to a faster, friendlier and easier way to find local businesses—the Internet.

While the Internet is the bane of the yellow pages' demise, with a 72.11% market-strangling hold on Internet searches, it is Google that is leading the way.

Simply put, Google has become the new "yellow pages." When you compare their market-dominating 72.11% of all Internet searches to their nearest competitor, Yahoo, with an unremarkable 14.57% of Internet searches, the case is made that every local business should concentrate all their Internet marketing efforts on Google and Google alone.

Let's face it. If your business does not show up on Google, you are invisible to the world, and if your business can't be found on the first two pages of Google, you (almost) don't exist because 83% of Google searches do not make it past the bottom of Google's second page.

This book will show you how to dominate your local competition with a high ranked, fully optimized listing in the prominent Google Places/Google Maps search engine results.

This book will walk you through the steps needed to optimize your Google Places listing through several simple techniques that work together to create an overall, competition-crushing strategy. The combination of these techniques is greater as a whole than is the sum of its parts...and while you can surely skip some of the seemingly small techniques that make up part of this strategy, it will subtract from the dominance you gain by employing all the steps together.

Traditional SEO

Traditional SEO can be powerful for your business, but is very time consuming. It is a moving target that changes dramatically all the time, literally shaking things up and turning the search results upside down every six months or so. It is something that is extremely valuable to your business, but something you will want to hire a professional to help you with.

If you own a business and that business relies on a customer base in your local area, at least start to join the Local Search revolution with the methods we lay out in this book, and then consult someone that can help take you to the next level.

Take a look at these stats:

73% of all online activity is related to local content (Google)

66% of Americans use the Internet to find local businesses (Comscore)

54% of Americans have replaced their phone books (yellow pages) with Internet searches (Comscore)

82% of local searchers follow up with their search by phone call and/or walk-in (TMP / Comscore)

43% of search engine users are seeking a local merchant with the intent of
buying in their local area

Local Search is the Answer

As a local business, you have a huge, wide-open opportunity to dominate your local competition by getting a free, prominent listing at the top of Google, using Google's local search features. Google has spent a large investment on becoming the most relevant search engine to its users, as Google understands that if you live in Las Vegas and you do a search for pizza, they know you want a pizza place in Las Vegas—not in Detroit.

This book is the ultimate secret weapon for local businesses to climb to the top of Google search results in their area. Forget about traditional SEO and expensive pay-per-click (PPC) advertising. Local

Search is king…and getting your business listed on top of Google's local search features is absolutely free, making your investment into this book a complete "no-brainer."

Understand that the information I share in this book is the same information that I follow (step-by step) for my clients, who happily pay me to keep their business at the top of Google's search results…and it's the same information I share in my marketing seminars.

Nothing is left out.

The book you hold in your hands was not written to sing the praises of local search, but instead, it was written to help you dominate your competition in your local area through local search using step-by-step, actionable methods.

Simply put…if you can follow step-by-step instructions, this book will teach you how to open the virtual floodgates of more business through new leads, increased sales, more visibility and additional customers.

Chapter 1

WHAT IS LOCAL SEARCH?

You have likely noticed recently that when you do a search on Google, often times your search results include a local area map with several local business listings next to it. These listings are easily identified because they contain prominent map markers next to each of those listings. These listings are also easily noticed because Google places them at the very top of the search results.

So just how does Google determine if a search has local intent?

1. The searcher uses geographic modifiers: instead of a search for "plumber," the search includes a specific location to specify the location for which they are seeking a plumber: "Detroit plumber" or "plumber in Detroit."

1. Google uses your IP to determine your location and returns results based on their estimate of your location coupled with what they determine to be a query with local intent.

This happens when Google identifies your search as originating from a specific place (or a specific place is made as part of the specified search) and that search includes a Google local search category for that geographic area. These results come from the Google Maps database.

As you can see on the screenshot on the preceding page, I did a search for a "place" that included a "business category" recognized by Google. Google, in turn, returned relevant, local businesses listings relating to my search. More importantly, these results are at the very top of the search results!

Studies have shown repeatedly that being at the top of Google correlates with more traffic, more exposure, more authority and more business. If you own a local business, this is where you want to be. In the days when the yellow pages were the dominating "go to" source for finding local businesses, this top Google maps listing is the equivalent to a full color, full page listing.

Local search can best be described as any online search that replaces a traditional search involving the local phonebook's yellow pages. Local search is often categorized as a search being made with the intention on finding something (business, product, service) in a specific geographic. More specifically, local search can be identified by searching online for a transaction that will occur offline in one's local area.

More simply put, if you live in San Diego and you do an online search for a plumber or a pizza, the search engines understand that you want to find a plumber or pizza in the San Diego area—not in Detroit! Because the search engines know where you are (using your IP address) they can now dish out the most relevant information for your search term.

In an effort to provide the most relevant information to you, Local Search has become of great importance to the search engines. Here's why:

According to Google, 73% of all online activity is related to local content.

1/3 of mobile search is locally based (Google).

According to ComScore, 66% of Americans use the Internet to find local businesses.

ComScore also reported that 54% of Americans have replaced the phonebook with the Internet for their local needs and that 82% of the people follow up with a phone call or a walk-in to the business they found through local search.

Quite simply, the name of the game for the search engines is RELEVANCY. The search engine that can be the most relevant, will likely be the most used search engine...and where the eyeballs go, so does the advertising dollars.

Over the past few years Google has become and remained the most dominant search engine on the planet. I would argue that this for no other reason than the simple fact that Google returns the most relevant information for any given search term.

The biggest concern of Google is to be the most relevant search engine to their users. This comes first to Google. Being the most relevant makes Google the "go to" search engine on the planet. Being the "go to" search engine means more customers, which in turn, makes them the "go to" source for advertisers.

I have seen Google end people's ability to support their families because these people tried to "out-think" or "out smart" Google, in an attempt to make

Google see their website or advertisement as "relevant" when it really was not. Google takes no nonsense from suspected scammers who try to "mess" with their system.

The point I am trying to make is that Google strives first to be the most relevant. Making money comes next (naturally) after being the most relevant. For purposes of this book, you need to think "relevance" first—just as Google does. When you first try to be the most relevant to your customers, Google will reward you with higher rankings.

As I mentioned in the Introduction of this book, Google commands an incredible 72.11% market share of Internet searches. While Google continues to gain market share, its biggest competitors continue to lose their share of the search market at double-digit rates. It is because of these statistics that this book will focus on getting your business at the top of Google— specifically Google Places/Google Local Maps.

Chapter 2

Google Places

Google Places is a revolutionary and totally free service that can literally catapult a small, local business from obscurity to insane profitability almost overnight. By taking advantage of a Google Places listing, you can highlight your business' products and services and place your information in front of thousands of local customers who are searching for your particular type of business in your particular local area through Google.com.

Not only will a listing on Google Places make your business stand out among dozens (sometimes hundreds) of local competitors, you will also get to tell potential customers a little bit about your business, where your competition cannot.

Because Google Places is relatively new, many businesses do not know about it and because of that, your competition probably doesn't know about it either! Right now, you have in your hands the ultimate "secret weapon" to gaining a stronghold in your local market—a weapon to not only getting a free, Google Places listing for your business, but inside tips, tricks and secrets to securing a front page listing for your business so that your potential customers are finding you—not your competition—when they conduct a Google search for your particular products and services in your area.

Love them or hate them, Google rules the Internet with over 280 million unique searches a day, coupled with a 72% + market share of Internet searches. With that kind of action, to me it makes sense to focus all of my SEO energy on only Google.

The purpose of this book is to show you how to claim your Google Places listing and then how to optimize that listing so that you—not your competition—is found first when your customers look for your products and services on Google.

In April 2009, Google announced that Local Search would start to show up more regularly in the "regular" search engine results pages, and since then, Google has delivered. Now, when you type in "plumber" or "pizza," Google serves up prominent, top of the page local listings that are relevant to your search terms.

Before Google Local, many businesses paid a fortune on Pay Per Click (PPC) ads to promote their businesses locally. Since Google Places (formerly Google Local Business Center) came on scene, however, online advertising costs for local businesses were able to be dramatically minimized by replacing PPC with a prominent Google Places listing. In my opinion, a Google Places listing is a much more prominent listing for those searching for local businesses than is their paid advertisement counterparts (on the right side of the Google page). Additionally, Google Places listings, being free, gave many local businesses an opportunity to compete with their deep-pocketed competitors who could afford to pay for expensive PPC ads.

Local business results for **plastic surgery** near Beverly Hills, CA

(A) Jon A Perlman, MD FACS **Beverly Hills Plastic Surgery**
www.perlmanmd.com - (310) 854-0031 - 11 reviews

(B) Robert Rey M.D.
www.drrobertrey.com - (310) 205-3107 - 9 reviews

(C) **Plastic Surgeon** Dr. Stuart A Linder
www.drlinder.com - (310) 275-4513 - 96 reviews

(D) Liposuction **Beverly Hills**
www.nathannewmanmd.com - (310) 273-3344 - 13 reviews

(E) Bedford **Plastic Surgery Center** Leaf Norman MD
www.plasticsurgery90210.com - (310) 274-8001 - 3 reviews

(F) **Beverly Hills Plastic Surgeons,** California Surgical Institute
www.californiasurgicalinstitute.com - (310) 275-1662 - 8 reviews

(G) Gotham Daniel S MD **Plastic & Reconstructive Surgery**
www.drgolshani.com - (310) 274-3481 - 5 reviews

More results near Beverly Hills, CA ›

When your business is listed in Google Places, it will show up on the map feature when a local search-er (in your area) does a search for your business' products and/or services. As you can see in the above photo, the Google Map listing (local business results) is very bold and they stand out like a colorful "sore thumb" on the Google search results.

On April 20th 2010, Google Local Business Center made another major move and became Google Places. Here's an excerpt from the official Google Blog, announcing the change:

4/20/2010 05:00:00 AM

Today the Local Business Center is becoming Google Places. Why? Millions of people use Google every day to find places in the real world, and we want to better connect Place Pages — the way that businesses are being found today — with the tool that enables business owners to manage their presence on Google.

We launched Place Pages last September for more than 50 million places around the world to help people make more informed decisions about where to go, from restaurants and hotels to dry cleaners and bike shops, as well as non-business places like museums, schools and parks. Place Pages connect people to information from the best sources across the web, displaying photos, reviews and essential facts, as well as real-time updates and offers from business owners.

Google Places is more than just a name change. Instead, Google Places offer more tools to local business owners to increase their visibility online. These new tools include the following:

Service Areas: If you travel to serve businesses, you can now include your service areas on your Google Places page. Additionally, if you operate without a storefront, you can now privatize your business address, which was not allowed in the past.

New Simple Ways to Advertise: For $25 a month, Google now allows you to add tags to make your listing stand out on Google.com and on Google Maps.

Free Photo Shoots: Google now offers a free photo shoot service, where Google photographers come to your business to take interior shots for you to include on your Google Places listing.

Customized QR Codes: Google will now create a custom QR code that is unique to your business. This code can be placed on business cards and other marketing material. These can be scanned by a smartphone which can take the customer directly to your Google Places page.

Real Time Updates: You can now update your Google Places page and have those updates appear instantly on Google.

Personalized Dashboard: Google provides your Google Places page with customized information collected through search. This includes providing data to you that tells you how many visitors visited your listing and what search terms they used to get there.

Chapter 3

Ranking Considerations

The information in this chapter has not been officially verified, as Google keeps tightlipped about their algorithms and the way they operate. This information is, however, quite accurate based on my testing, research and study.

As mentioned before, your business will benefit by being relevant in Google's eyes. The more relevant your business appears—the better rankings your business will get on Google Places. The key to this book is to show you what makes your business more relevant to Google.

Trust is a major factor that Google considers when ranking your business. So, the likely question that comes to mind is, how do you go about gaining Google's trust.

When you claim your business' listing on Google Places, you go through either a telephone or mail verification. This must be done as your first step in gaining Google's trust. While this is a step in the right direction, it is not going to give you automatic credit above your competition. You need to do more.

Business Data: if your business is not on Google Places but can be found elsewhere across the Internet, having the same or similar information about your business, Google will assign your business more trust. This includes documents that may be found on the Internet regarding your business: US Patent Application 20060149800, which is assigned to Google, demonstrates this:

> Abstract: A system determines documents that are associated with a location, identifies a group of signals associated with each of the documents, and determines authoritativeness of the documents for the location based on the signals.

Business Website: A website is not required to be listed on Google Places, but having a locally based website with search terms that are locally based for your business will surely factor in ranking your business on Google Places. It will really improve your chances of ranking higher.

Other Directories: Being listed in vertical, local, top tier and 2ⁿᵈ tier directories will be a major factor in Google's trust in your business. With listings in other directories, Google's trust in you will be greatly enhanced, as you will appear more likely to be a "real" business.

Reviews: It is hard to determine how much of a role reviews play in ranking your local business in Google Places, but reviews do play a factor. In my experience, the more reviews you have, the more trust Google will give you. This trust seems to relate to ranking as well.

Citations: citations are mentions about your business on other websites. In traditional SEO, to rank higher in the search engines, it is imperative to have links that link back to your website. The more quality, relevant links you have linking to your website—the higher you will rank. With local search, citations replace links.

Optimized Website: As mentioned before having a website is important to helping you get a high Google Places listing. If you have a website you will want to make sure it is optimized correctly for the search engines as this has also really shown to improve the Google Places listings along with giving your site a chance to show up in the regular Google results as well. This literally can double your exposure which helps you stay ahead of your competition. If you have questions on optimizing your website you will want to consult with a local Internet marketing consultant.

There is more to creating a relevant Google Place listings and in further chapters, we will address all of those factors.

Chapter 4

Claiming Your Google
Maps/Places Listing

Before you do anything else, you need to find out if your business has already been claimed on Google Places. This is something you or someone in your business would have to have done because it does require you to go through a confirmation process. Until recently, Google only allowed confirmation by mail. Now, they offer instant verification by way of callback service right to the telephone number you select.

Understand that your business may be able to be found on Google, but that does not mean the same as being "listed" with Google Places. The fact that you can do a search for your business name and see 10,000 results showing up that contain your business name, does not mean your business has been claimed. Many make this mistake and tell me, "Oh, my business is already on Google, when in fact, it is not listed with Google Places.

So, let's see if your business has been claimed…

Here's the method I use for all my clients and my own business as well. It's a quick and easy way to see if your business has been claimed or not for a few of the major directories. It even provides you with a score relative to your business on the Internet in terms of being officially listed or "claimed" in those directories.

Simply go to this website: http://www.getlisted.org where you will find a screen similar to this:

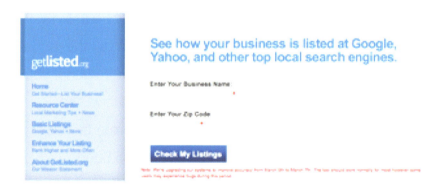

As you can see, this site is pretty self-explanatory. All you need to do to see if your business has been claimed is to type in your business name and the zip code to where your business is physically located.

In this example (next page), I randomly typed in "Beverly Hills Plastic Surgery" with a zip code of "90210." As you can see, a business was found under this name. Also, as you can see, this cosmetic surgery business has not claimed their Google Local listing (nor Yahoo, Bing, etc). This particular Plastic Surgery Business is leaving a great deal of money on the table by not having their business listing claimed.

Also, you will see that getlisted.org gives you a "listing score." In this case, getlisted.org assigned "Beverly Hills Plastic Surgery" a score of "0%" because the business has failed to claim a listing online.

Keep in mind that the higher the score, the better for your business as it is more likely to show up when people in your area are searching for your products and services.

Beverly Hills Plastic Surgery

9025 Wilshire Blvd
Beverly Hills, CA 90211
(310)888-0086
www.plasticsurgerybh.com

Listing Score: **0%**

This listing is 0% complete.
What does the score mean?

Expecting to see a different business?
Try our Advanced Check»

This again goes to show you that your business may be found on Google (this one shows the business address, phone and website) but not be listed in Google Local or Google Maps.

This means that when someone in the Beverly Hills area types "plastic surgery" or similar related search terms like "liposuction" etc, this business is not as likely to show up in Google Local/Google Maps.

Here's a look at the front page of Google when I type in "Beverly Hills Plastic Surgery." Also remember that if I were actually on my computer in Beverly

Hills, Google would know my location and would show these same results if I only typed in "Plastic Surgeon."

If our particular cosmetic surgeon has a copy of this book, he would easily be able to dominate this Google Map listing by knowing the secrets that you are about to learn.

Now, we will walk through getting listed in step-by-step fashion using a fictional business name.

Step 1: go to getlisted.org and enter your business name and zip code and click the "Check My Listings" box.

See how your business is listed at Google Yahoo, and other top local search engines

getlisted.org

Home
Get Started—List Your Business!

Resource Center
Local Marketing Tips + News

Basic Listings
Google, Yahoo + More

Enhance Your Listing
Rank Higher and More Often

About GetListed.org
Our Mission Statement

Enter Your Business Name:

Enter Your Zip Code:
90210

Check My Listings

Step 2: once we click the "Check My Listings" box, we come up with this:

NOT FOUND

ADDRESS NOT FOUND
CITY STATE ZIP NOT FOUND
WEB SITE NOT FOUND

Listing Score:

This listing is 0% complete.
What does this score mean?

 0%

Expecting to see a different business?
Try our Advanced Check+

⊗ Google
Business listing not found on Google.
Add your business listing

⊗ YAHOO!
Business listing not found on Yahoo.
Add your business listing

⊗ Best Web
Business listing not found on Best Of The Web.
Add your business listing

⊗ bing
Business listing not found on Bing.
Add your business listing

Why is it so important to claim your listing?

Step 3: From here, we will click "Add your business listing" that appears on the Google logo at the top of the page.

Note: While this book focuses on Google, it is important that you add your business with each of these listed. By registering with each one, Google will look at your listing as being more relevant and trustworthy, which is very important in your rankings.

Step 4: You should now be at the Google Places page, which should look something similar to this:

This is just a first step. Enter your business information here and watch your listing take shape on the right. In
service areas, and much more.

indicates a required field

Country: *   United States

Company/Organization: *

Street Address: *

City/Town: *

State: *   Select state

ZIP *

Note: You can hide your street address later if you don't want people to see it

Main phone: *

Example: (201) 234-5678   Add more phone numbers

Email address

Example: myname@example.com

Website

Example: http://www.example.com

☐ I don't have a website

Pacific
Ocean

Chapter 5

Setting up Your Google Places Listing

We will now get started into the strategy of setting up your Google Places listing for maximum effectiveness. You will need to go to this link below.

http://www.google.com/places/

First, you will need to click on the Places for Business link in the bottom right. Sign-in with your Google account after that. If you do not have a Google account, you will need to create one. You can do that here for free:

https://www.google.com/accounts/NewAccount

After you log in, your next step is to click "Add New Business." Begin entering your business information into the text boxes. It is best not to leave anything blank, as we will discuss in greater detail later.

For the most part, setting up this listing on Google Places is relatively straightforward. You will need to list the country your business is located in as well as street address, telephone number, etc.

The important point I would like to make here when entering this information is to keep it consistent with other information listed about your business on-line. If there is not much information online about your business, you will want to keep all future information you put online, consistent with your Google Places listing.

For example, if you list your telephone number as (619) 555-1212, do not list it elsewhere as 619-555-1212. If you list your business address as 223 Elm Street, do not list it elsewhere as 223 Elm St. If your zip code is listed as 90210-1101, do not later list it is 90210 (without the +4).

This consistency will help Google confirm that other mentions of your business online are, in fact, the same business as yours. Keep in mind that the more mentions of your business, the higher rankings you will get.

As you enter your business information, you will see the map move as it begins to find the location of your business as by the information you enter your business address.

DESCRIPTION

As mentioned, most of the information you will complete about your business is relatively straightforward. That is until you get to the description box. Here, I recommend a specific strategy involving the use of "keywords" relative to your business.

A "keyword" is a word or phrase that your customer uses to find you. For example, when my water heater blew up last month and was leaking water, I used the keyword, "Las Vegas Water Heater." Now, that may sound obvious, but what if you are an attorney practicing solely in Family Law? You do not want your description to read, "San Diego Attorney" but rather, you would want to focus on the keyword that your customers would use specifically to find you. In this case, I would likely use, "San Diego Family Law Attorney" as my primary keyword. But…I would expand on that to include other keywords as well. In this case, I would write something like this: "San Diego family law attorney practicing exclusively in child custody, child support, divorce and adoption." This way, I am hitting on other related keywords that deal with my profession, such as child custody, child support, etc. Google will put these keywords together and dish them out when your customer looks for you, but you need to do your part.

Now, that being said, it is important that you do not spam the "description" box. Many "newbies" coming along to set up Google Places listings often will resort to taking an approach similar to this: San Diego attorney, San Diego family law attorney, San Diego child custody attorney, San Diego divorce attorney, etc. In my experience, Google sees this as SPAM and you will be penalized rather than rewarded with a higher rank listing. It is important that your description reads like a coherent description of your business. With a little effort on your part, you can nail the description and still use good keywords.

CATEGORY

In the "Category" box, you will enter your targeted keywords and keyword category phrases. For the most part, Google will attempt to find a matching keyword phrase for your business and this is fine just as long as the keyword suggestion matches that of your business. For the main category, Google now requires you to select at least one of their suggestions. After that, you are free to type in your own category 9Google allows five category listings).

If Google does not find a match for keywords that correlate to your business, you can "free text" your "category" yourself.

For example, if you happen to be a business that sells office cubicles and your customers find you by using the keyword phrase, "office cubicles" or "Seattle office cubicles" you will see that Google does not have a category for this. Instead, they will suggest the category of "Used Office Furniture Store." Obviously, this will not work as your primary category. If someone wants to buy office cubicles, they are going to do a search for "cubicles" or "office cubicles" of "cubicle sales" etc.

Because Google requires you to use at least one of their suggestions, you will need find the one that best matches what your customers would be looking for.

Obviously, in the case of brand new office cubicles, the Used Office Furniture is not exactly the right category. So, instead you may want to use the Office Furniture category store or something similar.

After entering in your primary category, you will see that Google allows you to "add another category" with a link below the "category" box. Here, you can start using your own targeted keyword categories like "office cubicles" etc.

I highly recommend you add as many categories as possible. The more keyword targeted categories you use, the more chances you will get to have Google lead potential customers to you.

You can change this later, so do not fret if you find a better keyword to use later.

After completing the category section, you will click "Next" and you will be taken to a screen to complete even more details about your business.

The first one is:

SERVICE AREAS AND LOCATION SETTINGS

This is a new feature with Google as before, they did not offer traveling type businesses to expand their areas and list their business availability in other cities.

If you do have a business that travels to provide service in nearby areas, this is a great feature. Google will ask you to either give a service range in miles or you can list service areas by name. In this category, I prefer to list areas by name. This is because if I am operating a plumbing repair business in Escondido and I list Escondido as my service area, there is the chance that if someone in Chula Vista type in plumbing repair, that my listing may show there.

The next categories will be specific to your business hours and methods of payments. These are straightforward and again, I highly recommend that you do not skip any categories. Remember, we are trying to create the most RELEVANT listing possible.

PHOTOS

This is perhaps the most neglected category in setting up a listing on Google Places. From my experience, photos help increase your relevance. Now that Google is offering a free photo shoot of your business, I think this category is more relevant than first imagined.

Google allows for 10 photos of your business. Is Google going to check to make sure photos of your law firm or pizza parlor are photos of your law firm or pizza parlor? No, of course not. But, Google will know that you have 10 photos, so be sure to upload all 10 photos here. Remember, you can always go back and do this later.

When you do upload photos to your Google Places listing, I highly recommend you naming those photos using keywords. For example, I would change the name of my photos on my computer before uploading to: san-diego-pizza.jpg, seattle-attorney.jpg, las-vegas-plumber.jpg, etc.

VIDEOS

Videos are used even less than photos because most businesses do not have or do not know how to make a video. I am going to offer a simple and free way to make a video for your business. Again, put as many videos as you can on your listing.

Ok, a simple, quick and free site to make a video for your Google Places listing is at www.Animoto.com. At this website, you can choose free video. They have music you can use as well as photos, etc. You can also upload your own photos to include in the video.

Animoto will make a cool looking 30 second video that you can upload not only to your Google Places listing, but also to YouTube. We will get more into this in a later chapter. For now, it is important that you work on getting your Google Places listing filled up and looking very RELEVANT to Google.

ADDITIONAL DETAILS

Here, you can again use your keywords where possible, but again, do not SPAM.

If I were an attorney, I may offer addition details like the type of law I practice. If I were a plumbing repair place, I may offer details about product names or repair services.

For example (attorney):

Family law: yes
Divorce: yes
Custody: yes

Example (plumbing repair):

Water heater repair: yes
Toilet repair: yes
Pipe replacement: yes

Continue to add these additional details until you have your keywords covered. I am not sure where the limit is on this, as I have never reached it. It appears that Google allows far more than 10 "details" so use as many as you need.

Keep in mind that the more you can use your main keyword, the better, but without spamming. For example, if you can use your keyword in your business name or website name, that will help with relevancy. I know this is not always possible, but something to think about when you are getting started.

You will now click the "Submit" button and Google Places will take you to a verification page. From here, you will be given the option to verify your Google Places listing by either telephone or by the business address you entered for your listing.

Telephone recommendation is highly recommended here as postcard mail verification takes 2-3 weeks. During telephone verification, Google will make an automated and immediate telephone call to you with a PIN # that you will have to enter into your Google Places listing. Once this is done, you will be verified and your business will be located on both Google Places and Google Maps! But…there is more work to be done because we aren't just looking for a listing…we are looking for a top listing that completely dominates your competition. With that, let's move on…

Chapter 6

Reviews

In my experience, reviews are an important fact in determining relevance with Google. The more reviews you can get for your business—the better.

But beware…

I've seen people get burned by trying to fool Google, by making up all kinds of fake reviews themselves. Understand that Google places "flash cookies" on your computer and they know who you are and where you are. Don't think for a minute that if you log out of one Google account and log back in with another that Google does not know it's you. They do know!

So, don't make the mistake that many do. Do not review your own business—at least not from any Google account that you have ever used on your computer in the past.

If you must review your own business, do it from a completely different computer, under a brand new account that has never been used by you…and use a computer outside of your home or business so the same IP address is not identified by Google.

An easy way to get reviews for your business quickly is to send an email. Google Places makes this easy.

To do this, go to your Google Places page and click on the link that reads, "see your listing on Google Maps." This will take you to your Google Maps listing.

Now, up in the right hand corner of your screen, you will see a picture of the map that depicts your business' physical location. Above that is links to print, email or get a link. If you click "email" a link containing your Google Maps listing will automatically show up in an email.

From here, you can send an email to your past clients, friends, family members or anyone that can give your business a review. They will need a Google Account (Gmail, etc) to do this, but it only takes a few minutes to make a Gmail account and to give you a review. If they already have a Gmail account, it will let them write a review right away.

Here's the email I send out. You can use this or alter it to suit your needs:

Hi <name>,

(Google.maps link here)

I have recently updated my business information on Google and I would greatly appreciate it if you could visit the above link and write me a stellar review.

If you don't already have a Gmail account, you can set one up in under a minute.

I really appreciate your support!

This should get you some reviews. With these reviews, your relevance with Google will begin to grow. Remember, the more reviews you can get—the better so be sure not to skip this.

Chapter 7

Google Services

I do not have any data on this whatsoever, but I have read that Google may attribute more relevance to you when you include their services.

COUPONS

One of these services is the Coupon function that is in your Google Maps page. I do suggest you include some type of coupon in your listing as because it provides a webpage reference that adds authority to your business link.

Coupons are very easy to create. All you need to do is type in some text. If you want to get advanced and include a photo, this is easy to do as well.

To get to the Coupon function, you will see two options at the top of your Google Places page. #1 DASHBOARD and #2 COUPONS. All you need to do is click on the COUPONS tab and you will be brought to the page where you can make your coupon.

See screenshot example on next page:

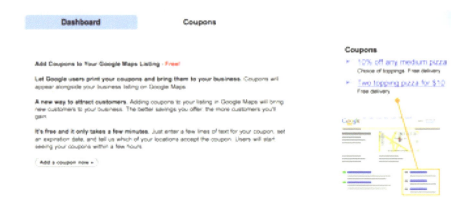

From here, you just need to click on the "Add Coupon Now" button and that will take you to the Coupon construction page.

From here, you just need to enter the information in the appropriate boxes and click "Continue." From there you will approve your coupon and it will go live.

GOOGLE CHECKOUT

Google Checkout is similar to PayPal in that it is an intermediary online payment processor. The SEO rumors are that Google will see your website as more relevant when you are using this service. Based on my study and what I have learned from other SEO experts, I do recommend using Google Checkout if you can.

Google Checkout is listed as a payment option when you enter payment options in your listing. I suggest you go back to your listing and click on the "Google Checkout" box.

If you would like to add Google Checkout as a method of payment, you can set up a Google Checkout account at checkout.google.com.

USER DATA

Go to Google.com and click "Maps." Now, for the sake of this example, type in something like "Seattle gyms." On the left side (in the 7-box), you will see a listing of gyms in Seattle. Click on the "more info" on one of those listings and it will take you to that Google Maps page. If you scroll to the bottom of the page, you will see "User Content." User content is information left that users have left in open collaboration. These Google users can add maps, reviews, photos, etc. The important feature here that I want to point out is adding a Map—basically, a map inside the map. I do not suggest you do this with your business Gmail account, however.

This feature will increase your relevance by showing that other people have "mapped" your location, usually indicating it is one of their favorite places. If you are a favorite among many, you will be a favorite to Google as well.

Here's how to add a map:

Go back to Google's Map page and sign in with an account that is not your business account.

Sign-in and click "Maps" then click again "My Maps" then click "Get Started".

What you want to do is create a map containing 'tagged' locations.

You can type in your business name and zip code and it will bring you to your listing.

Click the "Public Map" option then "Save".

Zoom-in the map at the location of your business listing. To add tags, click on the "tag" icon (the blue marker at the top of the map) and drag it to the right location on the map.

A window will appear for you to enter the "Title", type your business name in it. In the "Description" box, you can write any description you want but just be sure to include your business address and phone number just as it appeared in your Google maps listing. Then click "OK".

Your Google Maps listing will now display this user content you just added.

Get your customers, friends and families to do the same. This will help increase your relevance with Google.

Chapter 8

Becoming Relevant

Part of becoming more relevant to Google is by being trusted. Part of being trusted is being listed elsewhere on the Internet on websites that Google trusts.

To start earning this trust, you should begin by adding your business to other listing services besides Google. Google will cross-reference your information contained in other listings. When you list your business with other sites, you should include your address, phone number and all other information that is requested. Remember to keep this information consistent as stated earlier in this book, as you want every listing to look exactly alike so that Google counts that listing as being you and, in turn, ranks you higher.

Adding your business to other listings will move you up higher in Google's 7-box.

The websites that are included here are chosen because they are trusted by Google and because they are FREE. I highly recommend that you register at each of these.

Yahoo

Go to www.local.yahoo.com and scroll to the bottom of the page. Click "Add a Business."

Enter your business information and click "Submit."

Info USA

Register and setup. Click "Add Business Record". Fill in the information required then click "Submit". Select your business classification. Be sure to enter the same information as the one you entered in Google Maps local listing. Click "Submit."

A message is displayed informing you that it will take up to sixty (60) days for the business to get listed.

Remember: the information you include in the other listings should be exactly the same information for each listing or as close to it as possible.

Bing

Go to
https://ssl.bing.com/listings/ListingCenter.aspx

Click "Check Your Listing." Type in your business information. If the listing is not found, you will be able to log in with a Windows Live ID account (hotmail, etc). From here you can enter your business information similar to what you did when you set up your Google Places listing.

Yellow Pages.com

Go to http://listings.yellowpages.com. Click "Get your Free Listing Now". Search for your business by entering your phone number. Since it's not yet on the list, you can enter your business information. Click "Continue" button.

Choose the nearest category for your business. Narrow it down to a more specific category if possible. Click "Add Category" for every category that you have chosen. You are allowed up to five categories to add. Click "Continue" button.

Enter additional information as close as the information from the other listings you've created. Enter the "Access Code" then click "Create Listing". A new page will prompt you to create an account with Yellow Pages. Enter information and click "Register."

Super Pages

Go to www.supermedia.com and click "Free Business Listing" at the bottom of the page.

Enter your business phone number then click "Search." It's not yet on the list so click "Continue" button.

Enter your business information. From the "Choose Your Business Category", enter a category then click "Search."

Add all possible categories. There are no lim-
its as to how many categories to add. Click
"Continue" button if you're done adding categories.

Select as many products, services or brands
that are applicable to your business. Enter
your business hours, payment options, additional details, photos and coupon. Click "Pre-
view". If you like to upgrade for better listing,
you have to pay a certain fee. Click "No,
Thanks" to continue if you're happy with the
free listing.

A page prompts you to create your account.
Fill-in the information then click "Sign-in". Enter your account details then click "Continue."

The "Order Page" appears. Just check the "I
Accept" button below then click "Complete Order". The "Order Confirmation" page appears
confirming that the list has been added.

Local Eze

Go to www.localeze.com and click "List your
Business Today." From there, go to "Sign Up"
and enter your business information. LocalEze

usually takes a few weeks before you are listed but this is one of my favorite resources.

Navteq

Register at http://mapreporter.navteq.com/.
Enter your business address then click "Find".
It's not on the list so click "Click to add a drag-gable place marker on the map". Drag the place marker to your desired location.
Fill-in the "Point of Interest" (POI) information, then click "Submit".

Yelp

Go www.yelp.com and click "Business Owner" at the bottom page. Click "Get Started."

Search for your business name. It's not there so you can now "Add your Business to Yelp". Fill-in your business information like what you did with the other listing services. Click "Sub-mit."

Check your email to verify by clicking on the link provided.

City Search

Go to www.citysearch.com and search for your business name. If it wasn't found then click "Add Business." Enter your business information then click "Submit."

www.insiderpages.com
Go to www.insiderpages.com and search for your business name.

If it wasn't found then click "Add a Business". Click "Join Today" and fill your account and business information.

You can now "Claim this Business."

Other Directories

You can choose from other service listings below that are applicable to your business. The procedure is almost the same when adding a new business. Be sure to enter the exact information as those you have entered from the previous listings.

http://tripadvisor.com/

http://gayot.com/

http://ask.com

http://guidespot.com

http://zagats.com

http://fodors.com/

http://travelocity.com/

http://wcities.com/

http://hotelguide.net/

http://merchantcircle.com

Submit your business to as many listing services as possible so Google can find many references to your business online. This will give your business a better chance to appear in the 7-Box of its local listing.

After listing your business to several services, I recommend that you "social bookmark" all your business listings in each of these directories. Social Bookmarking is a way to publicly share your bookmarked websites and it is another way to make your business become more relevant in Google's eyes.

Start with www.socialmarker.com. Just have a copy of all your business listing URLs and bookmark it in as many social bookmarking sites as possible.

There are also paid listing services that remove the time and effort it takes for you to list your business at each individual site. My favorite is Universal Business Listings which can be found at www.UBL.org.

Here's what the UBL.org website says about handling this service for you:

Local Search Listing, Correction and Enhancement

The foundation of creating a business identity and marketing it is to first make sure the company's name, address, phone number and description can be found on Search Engines, online Yellow Pages, Social Networks, 411 Directory Assistance and Mobile/GPS navigation devices.

These local business searches are driven by databases of such listings, not from Website information. It is where 75% of all business searches take fewer experts know the tricks in dealing with 800-numbers, P.O.Box numbers and non-traditional phone lines.

These listings are becoming more important now that Search Engines and Mobile services deliver localized information based on knowledge of where you are when you conduct a Web search.

Sophisticated Web users know that you can submit listings directly to several of the larger Search portals, but this is time-consuming, complicated and few experts know all the places where the data needs to go. Unlike Web search, which is dominated by Google, searches for businesses are more likely to happen on other sites and Mobile phones. Even fewer experts know the tricks in dealing with 800-numbers, P.O.Box numbers and non-traditional phone lines.

UniversalBusinessListing provides a single entry point where you can create enhanced business profiles and for $30 a year that data gets distributed to all major outlets including:

> Search Engines such as Google, Yahoo, Bing Online Yellow Pages (Superpages, Yellow Pages, YellowBook)
>
> Social Networks such as MySpace
>
> Portals and Guides such as AOL MapQuest, CitySearch
>
> Cell Phones and Mobile (Blackberry and iPhone)
>
> 411 Directory Assistance
>
> In-Car GPS Navigation and Telematics such as OnStar
>
> UBL is effective because it feeds directly into

such databases as infoUSA and Acxiom that are used

as primary trusted sources by all major publishers. Listings from UBL are considered verified and are distributed to hundreds of sites directly and indirectly by this method.

In my opinion, UBL's service is well worth the $30 It costs!

Chapter 9

Geo Target Your Business With Photos

You can further increase your relevance by uploading photos of your business on public photo sharing sites. Specifically, these photos will be placed on maps at your business location.

There are two sites that I recommend and I will walk you through getting started on each.

Panoramio

Go to www.panoramio.com and sign-in (Sign-up for an account if you don't have one). Click "Upload your photos".

Click "Browse" for every photo to be uploaded then click "Upload" at the bottom of the page.

After successfully uploading all the photos, enter the title, tags and comment with your business name, tags and address as it appear in the Google maps listing.

To map the photos, click "Map this Photo" then map it to your business address. Click "Search" beside the address box then "Zoom" to make sure the photo is in the exact location you want (You can drag it to your desired location if it's not positioned there).

Then click "Save Position."

Repeat the process for all the remaining photos. Once finished mapping the photos, click "Save" at the bottom of page.

Flickr

Go to www.flickr.com. You can either create a new account or you can sign-in with a yahoo account.

Click "Upload Photos & Videos" then click "Choose your Photos & Videos" to pick up photos to be uploaded.

Be sure to click the "Public" option button before hitting the "Upload" button below the page.

Click "Add a Description" so you can enter your business name, address and tags the same as it is in the Google Maps Listing. Click "Save."

To map the photos, click a photo then click "Add to your map" on the bottom right pane. Click "OK", choose the "Anyone" option button as your "Default Permission". When your map is displayed, click the drop down arrow list at the bottom and choose "All your content" to display all your photos. Drag each photo to your targeted location.

Mapping photos on Panoramio or Flickr help by adding more content to your business listing in Google.

You can also Geo Target with webcams which will further add more content and more citations to your Google Places listing, but since most businesses do not incorporate webcams, I will not go into the details. If you are interested in pursuing this, however, a good place to start is www.earthcam.com.

Chapter 10

Citations

In traditional SEO, inbound links are critical to ranking well on the search engines. With Google's local algorithm—the one that is used to populate the 7-Box, Google Places and Google Maps, it appears that links and citations are becoming just as important as they are in traditional SEO.

In a patent owned by Google: Authoritative Document Identification, Google indicates the importance of physical location and how they tie citations to local businesses (U.S. Patent application #20060149800):

> Abstract: A system determines documents that are associated with a location, identifies a group of signals associated with each of the documents, and determines authoritativeness of the documents for the location based on the signals.

The patent information is quite a read, but in there, Google identifies what a document is:

"Document," as the term is used herein, is to be broadly interpreted to include any machine-readable and machine-storable work product. A document may include, for example, an e-mail, a web site, a business listing, a file, a combination of files, one or more files with embedded links to other files, a news group posting, a blog, a web advertisement, etc.

What this shows is that a "spiderable" link is not necessary for your business to receive a citation online. It now appears that a mention of your business online is enough to give you some attention from Google.

However, just like links, it appears that Google still places an importance on where the citation comes from. If a citation comes from the local Chamber of Commerce, it seems to carry more weight than if it comes from your sister's blog (although the blog will still hold some weight because volume is important too).

There are many ways to get your business listed apart from Google maps. The reason you should get listed in many places as possible is that you achieve more citations.

Citations make your business popular. The more citations you have, the more popular your business becomes. SEO calls this link popularity. Google and other search engines consider the number and quality of links you have when it comes to link popularity.

The idea is the same in local search. The mention of your business name in relation to your business location is important for you.

When Google finds that you are listed in other sites with the same business location, "trust" builds up and you become relevant in its eyes.

Now, what you want to do is start getting your business and it's location placed on local websites to increase the amount of citations you have with Google Places/Google Maps.

To do this, you should first do a Google search for business directory websites in your local area. For example, if you are a plumber in Seattle, do a search for "Seattle plumber directory" or "Seattle business directory" , etc. From the search results for this term, you should find good ideas to list your website.

In most cases, these types of websites will have a place for you to include your business information. If nothing is available, send them a request through a "contact us" link on the website.

Google will give you some serious credit if you are located on important websites like the Better Business Bureau and your local Chamber of Commerce websites because these are considered authoritative and because they have built-in trust. The drawback, however, is that these are often paid listings, although they are usually well worth the price you pay.

Remember to bookmark every webpage where your business is mentioned!

Chapter 11

Facebook

I don't think there is an off-page SEO book on the market that does not at least mention Facebook. The fact is, Facebook recently ousted Google as the number one most visited website. Because of that, Facebook is an important player online.

Although Facebook is widely considered to be used privately between friends and family, it is also a powerful way for businesses to connect more personally with their customers.

Facebook allows for Business pages and it is important that you start one for your business. Setting one up is fat, easy and painless.

If you have no Facebook account yet you may sign-up for one. It's easy and it's free. Once logged in, click "Advertising" at the bottom of the page. Click the "Pages" menu at the top of the page then click the "Create a Page" button at the right side of the screen.

Choose the type of your business, enter your business page name in the text box provided then click "Create Page."

If you need additional information, check out the help center. The help center has all the information you need about setting up your Facebook page.

To enter the basic information about your page, click the "View Page", click the "Info" tab then click the "Edit Information."

Once you have adjusted the settings, you can click "Save Changes." (Be sure to enter your information as it appears in your Google Maps Listing.)

Also be sure to add your website and target keyword phrases.

When you are ready to publish your page, simply click "Publish this Page". (You can make additional changes by clicking "Edit Page"). You can now add pictures. Your location should match your

Google map listing. The page name should also be the name you have on your Google map listing.

Chapter 12

Spying on Your Competition

To get a top ranking in the regular search results, one must have the most number of powerful incoming links. SEO calls it link popularity.

The same works with Google maps. To get to the top, one must have the most number of website citations.

The fastest and easiest way to determine how to beat your competition is by spying on their Google Maps listings and using that information to your advantage. Understand that they are not in the number one position by luck or happenstance. They are there because they are doing something that has made them appear to be more relevant than you in Google's eyes (their local algorithm).

Again, in almost all cases, it is simply the fact that they have more citations than you. However, volume is not always the case. Again, they may have a few less citations than you, but they may be listed on websites that Google deems more authoritative. As a general rule, go after the volume and revise later.

To see where your competition is receiving citations, all you need to do is go to their Google Maps page and scroll down to the category listed as "More about this place." This is where the citations for that business are listed. From here, you can visit these pages where your competitors are listed and try to get your business listed as well.

There are instances wherein a keyword phrase, say "Beverly hills cosmetic surgery", returns a 1-Box result when searched in Google although there are only a few citations. What made it to the top? It's because it had more reviews than the other competitors. If you keep an eye on the status of this keyword phrase everyday you will see that this will not stand in the 1-Box spot long because it does lack citations.

There are competitors that stay on the top position of the 7-Box although they don't have that much information like reviews, hours of operations, photos and videos, and other business information. What made them to the number one position? It's because they have the most number of citations listed on the Internet with their business name, business location and business phone number. Clearly it's these citations that got to them to the 1-Box or to the number 1 position in the 7-Box.

Bottom line? Go get your citations. Be sure to visit the citations of your competition and get mentioned on the same sites. Once you are listed on all the same sites that your competition is, go get more citations…and keep getting them. Go get more reviews…and keep getting them.

Adding citations and reviews on a regular basis will propel you to the top of the Google 7-box and perhaps even give you the royalty status of a 1-Box…and continuing to work on it will keep the competition at bay. This is how you dominate your competition and garner a ton of website visits, telephone calls and more traffic for your business.

Chapter 13

On Page SEO for Local Business

On-page optimization should begin as traditional SEO begins…and that is by building relevance through location + keywords. This is important for getting your website to also show up on the first page among the local listing sites we mentioned previously. Giving your business this added exposure is key to really getting the most out of your marketing efforts.

Keyword placement in your website should be considered a high priority and they should be used with a geographic slant.

Additionally, your full business name, address and telephone number should be placed on every page in your website. This again will contribute to better local rankings as well. It all works together for you.

There are many places where you can insert your target keyword phrase to optimize your site. It is always recommended that, at minimum, you include the primary target keyword phrase in the title of your website. It is also great if you can work your keyword phrase into your business name. The title of your website is known as the title tag. You will want to consult with a local marketing consultant that specializes in Internet marketing to help you ensure you get this part right.

For example, if you are a cosmetic dentist, the most likely keyword term used to find you would be, "cosmetic dentist." If you were based in Seattle and your actual business name was Brite Smile Dentistry, you would want to use a title tag similar to: Seattle Cosmetic Dentist, Mark Rogers DDS: Bright Smiles Dentistry. This way, your keyword is placed out in front and used as the business name. With the example I gave, you could still include your actual business name.

Besides the business name and website title, you should also include your target keyword phrase in your website's headline, main body text, footer, and meta tags.

Again, if you do not know how to do this yourself, I highly recommend hiring a professional Internet marketing consultant with SEO experience. They will know exactly what you're looking for and they can take the necessary steps to handle your on-page SEO so you don't take the chance of mistakenly altering something you shouldn't.

Bonus Chapter

Online Press Release Marketing

As you know publicity is an inexpensive way to promote your business and build major credibility for your company. Really any kind of exposure can help your business get in front of new prospects. Most businesses forget about the power of publicity, and even more businesses don't take note of the power of online publicity or online press release marketing.

A few well positioned press releases online can give your website more exposure in the search engines, add credibility to your business, build up your brand, help remove any negative publicity that may be lurking online, increase your incoming backlinks to your website, and ultimately help you get more customers.

When you can post information about your business in a high traffic area the only thing that can result ultimately is more traffic for you. This principal holds true with high traffic websites and press release sites are high traffic sources online that you can leverage to generate more traffic for your business.

When you submit or syndicate a press release online you can send it out to literally hundreds of press release sites if you want to. The more places you submit to the more benefit you will get. What I like about press releases is it does wonders for helping with branding. Since it is submitted to so many sites if you type in your business name after a press release is picked up in the search engines you will find a flood of results for your business. This results in making your business look important, plus it shows that your business seems to be active and thriving.

The Power of Positive Press Online

Sometimes businesses have some negative comments written about them online either from a customer misunderstanding or from a bitter competitor. You may never know where negative comments come up about your company, but there are solutions to calm the negative impact. Online press releases are sometimes used to again bring up more positive press about a business online and help overshadow tons of negative feed.

One other major online press release benefit is that they provide incoming backlinks to your website. As you know backlinks are super important and help you rank higher in the search engines. So the more links you get to your website, the better chance you have of showing up higher in the search engines than your competitors. Each press release you submit online can provide a backlink into your website.

Finally, if you position a press release correctly it can rank in the search engines on the first few pages for your main target keyword phrases. Including your target keyword in the title of your press release can give you a shot at seeing your press release rank and get direct traffic and more customers for you.

So now that I have sold you on press releases you probably want to know what is next, right? You want to know how to write them, where to submit them, and everything in between to ensure your online press campaigns are the most effective.

What Is A Press Release?

As you more than likely know a press release is an announcement of an event, performance, or other newsworthy item that is issued publicly. What most small business owners don't realize is how almost anything can be positioned as a press release online and used to generate yourself much traffic to your website, and potentially customers in your door.

Some ideas you could leverage to write a press release on include:

New Website Design

New Product Review

New Blog Post

An Opinion You Have

A press release just needs to have an

Press Release Structure

The key thing with any press release you write is to develop your angle first. The angle is the topic of your story, and covers the importance of who, what, when, where, and why. The first paragraph will typically lay out your main press release point or your angle. In a little bit I will show you an example of an opening paragraph so you can see this in action.

After the angle is created you will want to create a newsworthy title for your press release that includes your keywords in it. Try starting with your targeted keywords and include the angle of the release in the title or headline if possible to ensure the best chance of it getting accepted by the press release sites.

Below are a few examples of good press release titles targeting local keywords:

Tulsa, Oklahoma Chiropractors Adjusting The City

Sacramento Mexican Restaurant Offers Special
    Promotion for Veterans

Seattle Realtor Launches New Website

Miami, Florida Attorney Wins Monumental Case

Canton Florist Running Weekend Special Rates

After you create your angle and write the headline for your press release you need to create your introductory paragraph that lays out your press release point. This paragraph is the starting point for your release. As mentioned previously you cover who the press release is about (Example: your business), why you are writing the press release (Example: running a special sale), when the event runs (Example: Dates of Event), and how people can find out about it (Example: Website or Phone).

Below is an example of a press release opener.

"Tulsa, Oklahoma chiropractors are hard at work adjusting the city of Tulsa and a new website has been launched to highlight a Tulsa, Oklahoma chiropractor. The website, www.tulsaoklahomachiropractors.com, shares information and resources related to finding a good chiropractor for your next back or neck adjustment."

I hope you take notice that this press release just announced a new website and really didn't cover like a sale, employee hire, business event, etc. So hopefully you are beginning to see how you can position press releases to mean more exposure for your business online.

Now after the angle is created, the headline is written, and your opening paragraph is put together you will need to work on the body of the press release. This part includes 2 to 4 paragraphs. Typically the body of the press release just expands on the initial details covered in the opening paragraph.

So you can go into more details on the sale or more details on the features of the new website. Maybe talk about the reasons you hired the new employee. You can even talk about the location of the event in more detail, and things like that.

An easy way to create filler content is to come up with quotes that you can insert into these paragraphs as well. You can come up with a statement from yourself as the owner of the business that can be used here. It gives you a chance to maybe talk a little more about your business. I will show you a full sample press release below so you can see how the quotes are used.

Finally, you will conclude your press release with a closing paragraph or a call to action of some sort. This is the part of the press release where you give the readers a direct action. Most of the time this is to look at your website or call you. Since you are using this strategy to promote your website it will benefit you to put your website link, but if your business doesn't have a website yet just have people call your business to find out more information.

Press Release Example Here

Now as promised below I have copied a complete press release so you can see how all of this fits together. You can even take this press release and use it as a template if you would like.

------------------Begin Sample Press Release----------------
--

Tulsa, Oklahoma Chiropractors Adjusting The City

Tulsa, Oklahoma chiropractors are hard at work adjusting the city of Tulsa and a new website has been launched to highlight a Tulsa, Oklahoma chiropractor. The website, www.tulsaoklahomachiropractors.com, shares information and resources related to finding a good chiropractor for your next back or neck adjustment.

"Our goal with this website is to give website visitors access to a variety of information and resources related to finding and choosing the best Chiropractor in Tulsa, Oklahoma," said the owner of the website. "We understand that everyday increasingly people are going online to find information and find chiropractors in Tulsa, so we created this resource for them."

The site features a new design that allows for an easy way to find information and resources that will help in finding a reliable chiropractor in the Tulsa area.

The owner of the site also pointed out that a new article will be coming online soon that discusses the common myths people have with chiropractors. "Rumors and myths about chiropractic care has been floating around for years, and so hopefully this article will help shed some true light on this topic."

He mentioned that some of the myths people have are related to the safety of neck adjustments and the fact that people think you have to seek care for the rest of your life if you have a back issue. These concerns and more will be covered in the new article to be posted soon.

For further details on finding a good, reliable Tulsa, Oklahoma chiropractor can be found online at www.tulsaoklahomachiropractors.com.

-----------------End Sample-----------------

Submitting Press Release Online

Now that you have created a press release to promote your business online the next vital step is to submit that press release. There are literally hundreds of places online that you can submit your press release to which helps you build backlinks and increase your exposure which is so vital to your success with online marketing.

Here is a list of 5 free press release websites. This list is always changing, so I will also give you some searches you can run on Google which will bring back hundreds of free press release websites that you can submit to.

www.Free-Press-Release.com

www.prlog.org

www.pagerelease.com

www.1888pressrelease.com

www.onlineprnews.com

Now below I have a screenshot of a basic press

release website so you can see the basic layout of most press release submission sites. On each site you are looking for something that says "Submit Press Release" or something like that. Once you click on that you will typically need to register for the site with your name, email, and other basic information. Once you do that you just follow the instructions to copy and paste your press release onto the website.

As mentioned above you can also use Google to find even more press release sites to submit to on-line. Below are the common search strings I will put into Google to find all the press release sites I submit to currently.

free press release distribution

submit press release

press release submission

free press release website

submit press release free

Take a look at this screenshot for an example of a Google search you can run to find press release sites to submit to.

Press Release Promotion Conclusion

The best thing you can do with this strategy is submit your press release to as many online press release sites as possible to maximize your results. If you can create a release that you submit to 20 websites, just think of the additional exposure you would get by submitting to 50 websites. It can be a big difference.

This method is simple, but time consuming. Make sure you focus in on this method to get the best results possible.

Conclusion

This book is meant to be a resource that can be used repeatedly. The strategies and tactics detailed inside have been tested and proven to work for our clients virtually without fail.

If you follow the steps and take action, you can sit back and watch as your business climbs the ranks of Google Maps results and dominates the competition.

Remember, relevance is the key. Make your business relevant to Google through useful information, reviews, citations and a fully optimized Google Places listing and Google will reward you with higher rankings.

I wish you the best of luck and much more new business with your new, top Google rankings!

About The Author

Mike Griffin operates Louisville Marketing Labs and has been involved in Search Engine Optimization and Marketing since 2004. For more information and a free analysis of your website please visit:
http://www.LouisvilleMarketingLabs.com